THE 1980s

DECADE IN PHOTOS
THE TRIUMPH OF DEMOCRACY

Jim Corrigan

Enslow Publishers, Inc.
40 Industrial Road
Box 398
Berkeley Heights, NJ 07922
USA

http://www.enslow.com

Library of Congress Cataloging-in-Publication Data

Corrigan, Jim.
  The 1980s decade in photos : the triumph of democracy / by Jim Corrigan.
     p. cm. — (Amazing decades in photos)
  Includes bibliographical references and index.
  Summary: "Middle school readers will find out about the important world, national, and cultural developments of the decade 1980-1989"—Provided by publisher.
  ISBN-13: 978-0-7660-3137-1
  ISBN-10: 0-7660-3137-3
  1. United States—History—1969—Pictorial works—Juvenile literature. 2. History, Modern—20th century—Pictorial works—Juvenile literature. 3. Nineteen eighties—Pictorial works—Juvenile literature. I. Title. II. Title: Nineteen eighties decade in photos.
  E876.C69 2009
  909.82'8—dc22

                                                                                    2008052627

Printed in the United States of America.

092009 Lake Book Manufacturing, Inc., Melrose Park, IL

10 9 8 7 6 5 4 3 2 1

To Our Readers: We have done our best to make sure all Internet Addresses in this book were active and appropriate when we went to press. However, the author and the publisher have no control over and assume no liability for the material available on those Internet sites or on other Web sites they may link to. Any comments or suggestions can be sent by email to comments@enslow.com or to the address on the back cover.

Every effort has been made to locate all copyright holders of material used in this book. If any errors or omissions have occurred, corrections will be made in future editions of this book.

♻ Enslow Publishers, Inc., is committed to printing our books on recycled paper. The paper in every book contains 10% to 30% post-consumer waste (PCW). The cover board on the outside of each book contains 100% PCW. Our goal is to do our part to help young people and the environment too!

Produced by OTTN Publishing, Stockton, N.J.

TABLE OF CONTENTS

U.S. president Ronald Reagan (left) meets Soviet general secretary Mikhail Gorbachev in Switzerland, November 1985. During the 1980s, Gorbachev implemented new policies that allowed greater freedom in Soviet society. These would lead to the end of the Cold War and to the breakup of the Soviet Union in 1991.

WELCOME TO THE 1980s

The 1980s brought changes to everyday life. Personal computers were new. So were video games and music videos. Electronics were changing the way people worked and played. Important changes also took place in world affairs. When the decade started, the United States and the Soviet Union were still bitter enemies. Their rivalry would shift in unexpected ways during the 1980s.

For decades, America and the Soviet Union had competed in the Cold War, a worldwide struggle for allies and resources. Both nations wielded great power. More than once, the Cold War nearly exploded into direct military conflict. The threat of a nuclear war was always present. In 1980, the Winter Olympics became part of the Cold War rivalry. U.S. and Soviet teams faced off for a hockey game. Americans later dubbed it "the Miracle on Ice."

Rising rates of poverty and homelessness became major problems in America during the 1980s. The U.S. Department of Housing and Urban Development estimated that by 1987, at least half a million people were homeless.

The San Francisco 49ers were the decade's dominant football team. Led by star quarterback Joe Montana (number sixteen), the 49ers won Super Bowls after the 1981, 1984, 1988, and 1989 seasons.

Other uplifting events also helped restore American pride. The 1970s had been a hard decade for the United States. The country endured defeat in Vietnam, the Watergate scandal, and a fading economy. America bounced back in the 1980s. The economy improved. There were more jobs. The space shuttle made its very first flight, proving that America was still a leader in technology.

Yet the nation also experienced troubles during the decade. A dangerous virus called HIV emerged, causing tens of thousands of people to die from AIDS. A drug known as "crack" appeared on city streets. It was the source of much suffering and violence. In 1986, a space shuttle flight turned deadly. Seven astronauts perished. A year later, the stock market crashed. Meanwhile, wars raged around the globe.

As the 1980s continued, the Cold War began to thaw. In 1985, the Soviet Union gained a new leader. His name was Mikhail Gorbachev. He was unhappy with his country's condition. Soviet troops were losing the war in Afghanistan. In 1986, the Soviet Union suffered the worst nuclear accident in history. Gorbachev felt it was time to make changes. He wanted to overhaul the Soviet government and economy. He also wanted to improve relations with the United States.

U.S. president Ronald Reagan was a longtime critic of the Soviet Union. However, he welcomed Gorbachev's gestures of peace. For the first time in forty years, the end of the Cold War was in sight. Yet even bigger changes were happening inside the Soviet Union. Mikhail Gorbachev's reforms stirred people into action. They demanded more freedom and an end to communism. The various areas that made up the Soviet Union, called republics, began declaring their independence. As the 1980s ended, the Soviet Union was being torn apart. In a single decade, the world had changed dramatically.

Young people sometimes spent their free time trying to figure out puzzles like the Rubik's Cube.

MIRACLE ON ICE

The 1980 Winter Olympics were held in Lake Placid, New York. Ice hockey was among the most popular events. Most hockey fans expected the Soviet Union to win the gold medal. Soviet teams had triumphed in the four previous Winter Olympics. The Soviet squad was packed with veterans of international competition. The American team, by contrast, was made up of young college and minor-league players. In an exhibition game just a week before the start of the 1980 Olympics, the Soviet team had beaten the Americans by a score of 10–3.

On February 22, 1980, the teams faced off again, with a chance at Olympic gold on the line. Today, American hockey fans remember the game fondly as "the Miracle on Ice."

The opening ceremony for the thirteenth Winter Olympic Games, held in February 1980 at Lake Placid, New York. The Soviet hockey team had won the Olympic gold medal in 1964, 1968, 1972, and 1976. It was heavily favored to win again in 1980.

The American hockey team celebrates its 4–3 upset victory over the Soviets, February 22, 1980.

The match was more than a simple hockey game. It became a symbol of the bitter Cold War rivalry between the United States and the Soviet Union.

The Soviet team took an early lead. However, the young Americans stayed calm and played hard. The huge crowd cheered them on with chants of "U-S-A!" About midway through the final period, the Americans scored to tie the game at 3–3. A couple minutes later, team captain Mike Eruzione fired a shot past the Soviet goaltender. The American team managed to hold on. As the game ended, the American players—and the crowd—erupted in celebration. The American team went on to capture the gold medal. Their feat was a source of national pride.

Members of the U.S., Soviet, and Swedish hockey teams line up to receive their medals, February 24, 1980. The United States won the gold by defeating Finland, 4–2, in the finals. The Soviets defeated Sweden to earn the silver medal.

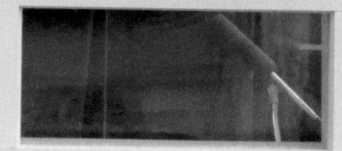

Ronald Reagan takes the oath of office as America's fortieth president, January 1981. In the 1980 election, Reagan easily defeated incumbent president Jimmy Carter. Reagan won forty-four states and 489 electoral votes to just six states and 49 electoral votes for Carter.

AMERICA BOUNCES BACK

*T*he 1970s had been a difficult time for America. The nation endured failure in Vietnam. A scandal called Watergate shook the government. In November 1979, more than fifty U.S. citizens were seized in Tehran, the capital of Iran, where they were held hostage.

The hostages in Iran were U.S. embassy workers. They had been taken prisoner shortly after a revolution in Iran. The new Iranian government and its supporters disliked America. They held the embassy workers captive to blackmail the United States.

An American lieutenant places flowers on a memorial to the eight U.S. soldiers killed during the attempt to rescue the hostages from Iran, April 24, 1980.

In April 1980, U.S. special operations troops were sent to Iran on a secret mission to free the hostages. In the first part of the plan, eight helicopters and six large transport planes were supposed to land in a desert area southeast of Tehran. Later, after American soldiers had stormed the embassy compound and freed the hostages, the helicopters would fly everyone out of Tehran. Unfortunately, the helicopters flew into a heavy sandstorm as they approached the landing site in the desert. Three of the helicopters were damaged. The five that remained would not be enough. The mission was called off. As the aircraft were preparing to leave, however, one of the helicopters crashed into a transport plane. It exploded, killing eight U.S. servicemen. The failure embarrassed the United States. It seemed that the misfortune of the 1970s would continue.

By November 1980, Americans were ready for a change. President Jimmy Carter was running for reelection. Voters chose his opponent, Ronald Reagan, instead. Reagan was sworn in as president on January 20, 1981. Only minutes later, Iran finally released the hostages. They had spent 444 days in captivity. The nation celebrated their safe return.

As president, Ronald Reagan helped America rise above the gloom of the 1970s.

Factory workers in many American industries struggled to make ends meet as their companies closed or shipped jobs overseas during the decade. This photo shows a shuttered steel mill.

A high-rise apartment building for low-income families stands in the foreground of this view of midtown Manhattan's skyscrapers, symbols of America's wealth. During the 1980s, the gap between the richest and poorest Americans grew wider. By 1989, the top 4 percent of American taxpayers (3.8 million individuals or families) earned as much as the bottom 51 percent (49.2 million individuals or families).

Reagan was nearly seventy years old when he took office. However, he showed an upbeat energy that people admired. For much of his life, Reagan had been an actor. He starred in dozens of movies and TV shows. His acting skills made him an excellent public speaker. In his speeches, Reagan talked about making America strong again. He said that the government had grown too big. It spent too much money and hindered business. Reagan also called for a stronger military. Listeners found his words inspiring.

America still faced many challenges. The economy was struggling. One in every ten workers had no job. Food, gas, and other goods were very expensive. Yet people sensed that a change was taking place. America was bouncing back.

PRESIDENT REAGAN IS SHOT

Secret Service agents surround President Reagan (left) after he was shot outside the Washington Hilton Hotel. Reagan's press secretary, James Brady, and policeman Thomas Delahanty lie wounded on the sidewalk.

On March 30, 1981, a gunman tried to kill President Ronald Reagan. The president was giving a speech at a hotel in Washington, D.C. Outside, a crowd gathered in hopes of catching a glimpse of Reagan as he walked to his waiting limousine. When the president emerged from the hotel, a man in the crowd pulled out a handgun and started firing. Reagan and three other people were hit.

Secret Service agents rushed the president to the hospital. Doctors treated his wounds. Within a month, Reagan was back at work in the White House. The ordeal made him even more popular with Americans. He had stayed upbeat even in the face of grave danger.

U.S. marshals escort John Hinckley Jr. to prison, 1981.

The other three victims also survived. But one of them, presidential aide James Brady, was left partially paralyzed. He became an activist for gun control.

The gunman, John Hinckley Jr., was captured immediately after the shooting. Investigators learned that Hinckley was obsessed with actress Jodie Foster. He thought that shooting the president would impress her. John Hinckley was put on trial but found not guilty by reason of insanity. He was placed in a psychiatric hospital. He remains in custody today.

Vice President George H.W. Bush and White House staff members pose in front of a "get well" message for President Reagan and the others injured in the attack, April 1981.

SPACE SHUTTLE BLASTS OFF

The space shuttle is different from other spacecraft. After launch, it can fly back to Earth like an airplane. That makes the space shuttle reusable. It can go on many missions. In 1981, America launched the world's first space shuttle.

The space shuttle is the one of the most complex machines ever built. It can carry huge objects into orbit. It supports life for up to seven astronauts. They do experiments in space, fix broken satellites, and perform other missions. When the job is done, the space shuttle returns to Earth and lands on a runway.

The space shuttle *Columbia* begins its first trip into space, April 12, 1981.

Astronauts John W. Young (left) and Robert L. Crippen work at the controls of the space shuttle. Young, the mission commander, had previously flown to the moon twice during the Apollo program. For Crippen, the pilot, *Columbia's* initial flight was his first time in space.

Columbia glides through the atmosphere after two days in space. During the mission, the shuttle orbited the earth thirty-six times.

The first working space shuttle was named *Columbia*. *Columbia* blasted off for its first mission on April 12, 1981. Anxious crowds cheered as the ship's powerful rocket boosters sent it into space. It was a proud moment for America.

Eventually, America's space agency—the National Aeronautics and Space Administration, or NASA—would add four more space shuttles to its fleet. However, two shuttles would be stricken by tragedy. *Challenger* exploded shortly after a launch in 1986. *Columbia* was lost during an accident in 2003. Both tragedies claimed the lives of all astronauts aboard. The remaining three shuttles are *Discovery*, *Atlantis*, and *Endeavour*. NASA plans to retire them in 2010.

Young and Crippen, wearing tan space suits, emerge from *Columbia* after landing the shuttle at Edwards Air Force Base in California, April 14, 1981.

MTV Changes Pop Music

Before the 1980s, music was mainly for the ears. Music lovers listened to records and the radio, but had little to watch. That changed in 1981 with the arrival of Music Television, or MTV. The new channel played music videos 24 hours a day.

MTV was an instant hit with young people. For the first time, they could watch pop artists perform their latest hits. A video jockey, or VJ, introduced

MTV's original VJs included (left to right) Nina Blackwood, Mark Goodman, Alan Hunter, Martha Quinn, and J.J. Jackson

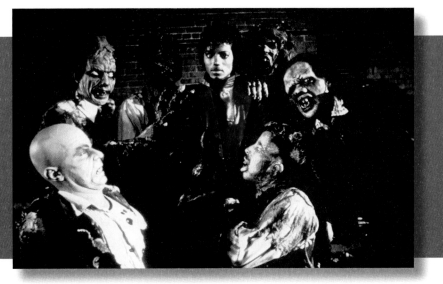

Pop star Michael Jackson is surrounded by ghouls during the 1983 video for his hit song "Thriller." During the 1980s, Jackson sold more albums than any other performer, thanks to such hits as "Beat It," "Billie Jean," "Bad," and "Man in the Mirror."

songs and talked about the performers. Early videos were simple. They showed band members singing and playing instruments. Later, videos became more elaborate. They told a story and featured special effects.

Certain performers quickly realized the value of the music video. It enabled them to build a personal image that matched their music. Madonna and Michael Jackson were among the first artists to make use of MTV. Jackson's dazzling "Thriller" video debuted in 1983. Its huge popularity made Jackson a superstar. It also made MTV a driving force in the music industry. Today, there are many music video channels. The original MTV now devotes most of its airtime to full-length television shows.

MTV helped to introduce hip-hop music to mainstream American audiences. The groundbreaking rap group Run-D.M.C. is pictured at the second MTV Music Awards show, September 1985.

REAGAN HEATS UP THE COLD WAR

By the 1980s, the Cold War was nearly four decades old. America and the Soviet Union remained bitter rivals. A nuclear war between the two superpowers always seemed possible. President Ronald Reagan wanted to show that America was determined to win the Cold War.

Reagan felt that the United States had to deal with the Soviets from a position of strength. He began building up the U.S. military. Under his administration, spending on weapons and other military projects increased

Soviet soldiers stand near a truck equipped to launch a small nuclear missile, 1982. During the Cold War, both the United States and Soviet Union built up their nuclear arsenals. The two superpowers each possessed thousands of nuclear weapons.

In the early 1980s, the United States began spending large amounts of money to develop new weapons, such as the B-2 "stealth" bomber. This aircraft's unusual design made it hard to see on radar. This would allow B-2 bombers to avoid air defenses if they had to attack the Soviet Union.

by tens of billions of dollars. In a famous speech, Reagan called the Soviet Union an "evil empire." He made it clear that America would not tolerate Soviet aggression.

At first, President Reagan's tactics caused the U.S.-Soviet rift to worsen. However, in 1985 a new Soviet leader took office. Together, he and Reagan would work to end the Cold War.

NEW SOVIET LEADER

Mikhail Gorbachev knew that the Soviet Union was crumbling. The Soviet economy struggled. Workers were restless. To make matters worse, the Soviet army was bogged down in a war in Afghanistan. In 1979, the Soviet Union had invaded that neighboring country. America was spending a huge amount of money on its military. There seemed to be no way the Soviet Union could keep pace. It appeared to be losing the Cold War. When Gorbachev came to power in 1985, he began making changes. He tried to improve the economy. He allowed more free speech. Gorbachev also began negotiating with the United States. His reforms would bring historic change.

U.S. Marines survey the remains of a barracks destroyed by a car bomb, October 1983. The American troops were in Lebanon trying to stop a brutal civil war that had been raging there since the mid-1970s.

DEADLY CONFLICTS AROUND THE WORLD

During the 1980s, limited—if often very brutal—wars raged all around the globe. In Afghanistan, Soviet troops battled fighters called *mujahideen* ("holy warriors"). The Middle Eastern countries of Iran and Iraq fought a ruthless war. Both of these conflicts lasted for most of the decade.

Two U.S. warships escort an oil tanker through the Persian Gulf, October 1987. During the Iran-Iraq War (1980–1988), Iran started attacking oil tankers from Iraq's Arab ally, Kuwait. The United States became involved to protect the Kuwaiti tankers and keep the oil flowing.

Other wars were much shorter. In 1982, Britain and Argentina fought a ten-week conflict. It was called the Falklands War. The Falkland Islands are located in the South Atlantic Ocean. Britain and Argentina both claimed to own them. (The Argentines call the islands las Islas Malvinas.) In April 1982, troops from Argentina invaded the islands. In response, Britain sent an armada of warships to the Falklands. Fierce battles erupted. In all, more than 900 soldiers and sailors died in the fighting. But the British forces won. Argentina surrendered in June. Nevertheless, the underlying cause of the war was never resolved. Today, both countries still claim ownership of the Falkland Islands.

The Reagans honor victims of the bombing of the U.S. Embassy in Beirut, Lebanon. More than sixty people were killed when a car bomb exploded at the embassy on April 18, 1983. Six months later, the U.S. Marine barracks in Beirut was destroyed by another bomb.

A cache of Soviet-made weapons seized by U.S. Marines during Operation Urgent Fury, the 1983 invasion of Grenada.

A civil war is a conflict between groups of people from the same country. For years, the country of Lebanon had endured a civil war. In 1982, soldiers from the United States and other nations went to Lebanon. They tried to bring an end to the fighting. Instead, they became targets. On October 23, 1982, suicide truck bombers struck the bases of American and French troops in Beirut, Lebanon's capital. The explosions killed 241 American servicemen and 58 French soldiers. The surviving peacekeeping troops were soon pulled out of Lebanon. The civil war continued.

Grenada is a tiny island nation in the Caribbean Sea, near the coast of Venezuela. In 1979, its government was overthrown. The new prime minister, Maurice Bishop, forged friendly relations with the Soviet Union and Cuba. American officials were not pleased. President Ronald Reagan said Cuba was planning to use Grenada as a base for spreading communist revolutions in Central America. He said Grenada posed a threat to American security.

In October 1983, Bishop was overthrown and killed by a group of army officers. An openly communist military government took power. President Reagan quickly ordered an invasion of Grenada. He claimed that American students at a medical school there were in danger. On October 25, the first U.S. invasion troops landed. Grenadian soldiers, as well as several hundred Cubans on the island, fought fiercely. But within a few days, American forces had defeated most of them and toppled the military government.

War on Drugs Widens

Drug abuse is a problem in many cultures. People who try illegal drugs risk their health, their families, and their freedom. In the 1980s, America experienced a surge in drug abuse. A new drug called "crack" had arrived.

During the 1980s, cocaine was a popular drug among young and wealthy people, such as professional athletes, Wall Street stockbrokers, and celebrity musicians and actors. In 1982, a government survey found that 22 million Americans had tried cocaine.

Crack is a form of cocaine. Cocaine is a white powder. Abusers typically inhale it. Crack is different. It is solid and abusers can smoke it. Unlike cocaine powder, crack is cheap. It costs just a few dollars. Despite health dangers that include heart failure, liver damage, and death from overdose, many abusers quickly became addicted to crack. By 1987, the drug had spread across the entire nation.

The crack epidemic created many problems. Hospitals strained to treat

Crack cocaine was a form of the drug that became very popular in the mid-1980s. It came in small hard chips, known as "rocks."

An agent of the Drug Enforcement Administration (DEA) arrests a woman for selling drugs.

an influx of overdose victims. Police struggled to contain a rise in crime. Rival drug dealers fought gun battles on city streets. Addicts robbed and stole so they could buy more crack.

President Reagan said that the nation needed to expand its war on drugs. Cities hired more police officers. New laws targeted drug crimes. Dealers would spend more time in prison if found guilty. TV ads urged young people to "just say no" to drug abuse. Gradually, the crack epidemic began to decline. Still, abuse of illegal drugs would remain a major problem in the United States.

First Lady Nancy Reagan speaks at an anti-drug event at the White House, 1986. Mrs. Reagan created a program called "Just Say No," which was intended to teach kids how to avoid dangerous drugs.

SCOURGE OF AIDS

A new disease emerged in the 1980s. Scientists named it acquired immuno-deficiency syndrome, or AIDS. The strange new disease proved deadly. It would go on to become a global epidemic.

AIDS is caused by a virus. It is called human immunodeficiency virus, or HIV. The virus makes a person's body unable to protect itself from other diseases. As a result, AIDS patients may suffer from many illnesses. A person can get the virus by having unprotected sex with an infected partner. Another way is by coming into contact with infected blood (for example, through the sharing of a hypodermic needle). Finally, an infected mother may unknowingly pass the virus on to her baby.

Hollywood stars Rock Hudson and Elizabeth Taylor appeared in several films together, including *Giant* (1956) and *The Mirror Crack'd* (1980). Hudson's AIDS-related death in 1985 made many Americans aware of the disease for the first time. After her friend's death, Taylor would become very active in the fight against AIDS, founding the American Foundation for AIDS Research (now called amfAR).

During the 1980s, AIDS was a major concern in the United States. Once people learned to be careful, the number of AIDS cases declined. Even so, an estimated 56,000 Americans still contract the virus each year. In other parts of the world, the infection rate is much higher. Scientists have yet to find a cure for AIDS. However, new drugs are helping AIDS victims live longer.

Ryan White was a boy from Indiana. He had a disease called hemophilia, which prevents blood from clotting properly. Ryan contracted HIV, either from tainted clotting medication he took or from a tainted blood transfusion. In 1984, as a thirteen-year-old, Ryan was diagnosed with AIDS. At the time, many people did not understand AIDS. They thought a person could get AIDS simply by being around someone with the disease. Parents and teachers tried to keep Ryan from going back to school. Ryan became a symbol of the AIDS epidemic. He died in 1990 at age eighteen.

This poster was inspired by the experience of Ryan White, a thirteen-year old hemophiliac with AIDS. When Ryan was not allowed to attend school in 1985, he became a symbol of the intolerance that people with AIDS faced.

I HAVE AIDS
PLease hug me
I can't make you sick

AIDS HOT LINE FOR KIDS
CENTER FOR ATTITUDINAL HEALING
19 MAIN ST., TIBURON, CA 94920, (415) 435-5022

Rise of the Computer

The first electronic computer was invented in the 1940s. It was the size of a building and worked very slowly. By the 1970s, computers were smaller and faster. However, they were still expensive. Only businesses could afford them. In the 1980s, computers became less costly. For the first time, a family could buy one for the home. The age of personal computers had arrived.

The Commodore 64 was released in 1982, and quickly became one of the most popular home computers. More than 30 million of these machines, which could be hooked up to a television, were sold during the mid-1980s.

Various companies developed home computers. Two eventually came to dominate the market: Apple and IBM. Two young men started Apple in a family garage. With clever ideas, they built their tiny business into a huge corporation. IBM, their rival, was already a huge corporation. For decades, it had pioneered the computer industry. Meanwhile, a small company called Microsoft began making programs for IBM's computers. Microsoft quickly became the world leader in software.

Hewlett-Packard introduced its first personal computer, the HP-85, in 1980.

The original Apple Macintosh, unveiled in January 1984, changed the personal computer industry. The Mac was the first computer to use a graphical user interface—a screen with small images, called icons, that could be clicked or moved to run programs. The Mac was also the first home computer to use a mouse. Both of these innovations would become standard on later personal computers.

By today's standards, computers of the 1980s were primitive. They had blocky graphics and little memory. The World Wide Web did not yet exist in the 1980s. Computer users played games. They also kept records and wrote reports. Computers made these tasks much easier.

In 1980, Bill Gates's small software company, Microsoft, developed an operating system called MS-DOS for IBM's first personal computer. MS-DOS became very popular. In 1985, Microsoft released a graphical version of the MS-DOS software, called Windows.

SPACE SHUTTLE EXPLODES

In 1986, disaster struck the U.S. space program. The shuttle *Challenger* exploded shortly after liftoff. All seven astronauts aboard *Challenger* were killed. America mourned their loss.

The accident took place on January 28, 1986. *Challenger* blasted off normally. A nearby crowd cheered the launch. Many more viewers watched on television.

The crew of the space shuttle *Challenger* included (front, left to right) pilot Mike Smith, mission commander Dick Scobee, Ron McNair, (back) Ellison S. Onizuka, Christa McAuliffe, Greg Jarvis, and Judy Resnik.

This photo was taken a few seconds after *Challenger* exploded shortly after liftoff. People watching the launch were shocked by the explosion. After fifty successful space shuttle missions, the launches had become almost routine.

The launch appeared to be a success. Then, just seventy-three seconds into the flight, *Challenger* suddenly blew up. A huge cloud of smoke hung in the blue sky. People stared upward.

An investigation pointed to a faulty seal on one of the shuttle's rocket engines as the cause of the explosion. The shuttle astronauts had no chance at survival. NASA did not launch another space shuttle for more than two years.

This damaged piece of *Challenger's* rocket motor was recovered after the accident. NASA investigators found that a damaged gasket in one of the shuttle's two rocket motors had caused the explosion. It was the deadliest accident in NASA's history.

CHALLENGER DISASTER CLAIMS TEACHER

Christa McAuliffe was a schoolteacher from New Hampshire. NASA chose her for its Teacher in Space Project. McAuliffe trained like an astronaut. She spurred public interest in the space program. The Challenger mission was to be her first flight in space. Like the other crewmembers, she died in the explosion. Christa McAuliffe was thirty-seven years old.

NEW TRENDS IN FASHION

The 1980s saw several distinct fashion trends. Styles changed during the decade. In the early 1980s, workout clothes were popular casual wear. Women wore headbands, leg warmers, and leotards. Men preferred tank tops and jogging suits. Brand-name sneakers became highly fashionable with both genders.

For business attire, men wore designer suits. They often slicked back their hair with gel. Women's clothing reflected their rising status in the business world. Shoulder pads helped project a powerful female image. Earrings and an expensive watch completed the look.

More than ever, rock stars and TV shows influenced fashion. Teenage girls dressed like Madonna. They wore black skirts with lace gloves and long necklaces. They teased up their hair with hairspray and added big bows. Young men copied the *Miami Vice* look. Stars of the TV police drama wore suit jackets over pastel T-shirts. They were

During the 1980s, many young girls tried to copy Madonna's fashion style and attitude. The pop singer was one of the decade's biggest entertainers, with hits like "Holiday," "Crazy for You," "True Blue," and "Like a Prayer."

As growing numbers of women were promoted to high-powered corporate jobs during the 1980s, power suits, with vivid colors and shoulder pads, became common. This fashion trend was reflected in popular television shows of the decade, such as *Designing Women*.

unshaven and wore no socks with their shoes.

The 1986 film *Top Gun*, which was about fighter pilots, made designer sunglasses trendy. The movie also added to the popularity of leather jackets. As the decade ended, rock music once again affected fashion. The ripped jeans and denim jackets worn by heavy-metal bands were in style.

Miami Vice was one of the most popular shows on television during the mid-1980s. The program had an influence on men's fashions during the decade.

Radiation emitted after a 1986 accident at this nuclear power plant in Chernobyl caused thousands of deaths.

NUCLEAR DISASTER in EUROPE

In April 1986, the entire world watched a small town called Chernobyl. The town was located in Ukraine, which at the time was part of the Soviet Union. A crisis was unfolding at Chernobyl. A nuclear power plant had exploded. It was burning out of control. Huge amounts of nuclear debris were escaping into the air. It was the worst nuclear power accident in history.

British newspapers announce the Chernobyl disaster, April 30, 1986.

All power plants make electricity by heating water to produce steam. The steam turns turbines, which then generate the electricity. Coal- and oil-fired plants burn fuel to produce steam. Nuclear power plants are different. They create heat by splitting atoms of an element called uranium.

The nuclear process is very efficient. Yet it can also be dangerous. A nuclear reaction produces radiation. Radiation can be harmful to humans and animals. Workers at a nuclear power plant must ensure that no radiation escapes. In 1979, there was a nuclear accident in Pennsylvania.

A small amount of radiation escaped from the Three Mile Island nuclear power plant. People living nearby were frightened. However, the crisis ended before anyone was harmed.

The accident at Chernobyl was different. Plant workers had become careless. They ignored safety rules. On April 26, 1986, two huge explosions rocked the power plant. Two workers died instantly. Then a massive fire started. The blaze spewed radiation into the air. Deadly particles drifted

Young patients at a Soviet clinic established to treat children suffering from leukemia caused by radiation from Chernobyl, circa 1989.

Children light candles in a park in Ukraine to mark the fourth anniversary of the Chernobyl accident.

through the sky. The fire burned for two weeks. Dozens of firefighters and plant workers died from radiation sickness.

The nuclear accident made Chernobyl unfit for human life. Residents of the town had to move. The radiation also affected nearby areas. Over 200,000 people were forced to leave their homes forever. Workers buried the damaged portions of the plant in cement. Scientists found that the wind had spread radiation to other countries in Eastern Europe. Some children who were near Chernobyl later became sick with cancer.

The Chernobyl disaster showed that nuclear energy requires extreme caution. Since then, nuclear power plants have become safer. Engineers learned from the mistakes made at Chernobyl. Today, nuclear power plants create roughly 15 percent of the world's electricity.

THE IRAN-CONTRA AFFAIR

Political scandals involve wrongdoing by government officials. The Iran-contra affair was a major political scandal in the mid-1980s. It rocked the presidency of Ronald Reagan.

In 1985, the Reagan administration secretly began selling weapons to Iran. This went against an American ban on arms sales to Iran. The ban had been in effect since the seizure of the U.S. embassy in 1979. However, President Reagan was hoping to get something in return for the arms sales. He wanted the Iranian government to pressure terrorist groups it supported to release American hostages they were holding in Lebanon.

President Reagan meets with Adolfo Calero (left), a leader of the Nicaraguan contras, in April 1985. Lieutenant Colonel Oliver North (center) stands in the background. Two years later, both Calero and North admitted their involvement in the Iran-contra affair to Congress.

A soldier aims a TOW anti-tank missile, circa 1985. The illegal sale of TOW and Hawk missiles to Iran during 1985 and 1986 brought in over $10 million. Those funds were secretly used to provide weapons and supplies to Nicaraguan rebels.

The arms sales to Iran generated millions of dollars in profits. Some of Reagan's aides decided to use those profits to support a group of rebels in the Central American country of Nicaragua. These rebels, known as the contras, were trying to overthrow the communist government of Nicaragua. Giving aid to the contras was against U.S. law.

In late 1986, details of the Iran-contra affair became public. In 1987, the U.S. Senate investigated the scandal. The hearings were aired live on national TV.

Eventually, eleven people were convicted of crimes related to the scandal. Two of the convictions were later overturned on technicalities. As for President Reagan, no proof emerged that he knew about the illegal funding of the contras. But the Iran-contra affair haunted Reagan for the rest of his time in office.

President Reagan discusses the Iran-contra affair with some of his top advisers, November 1986. Pictured are (left to right) Secretary of Defense Caspar Weinberger, Secretary of State George Shultz, Attorney General Ed Meese, White House Chief of Staff Don Regan, and the president.

BLACK MONDAY HITS THE STOCK MARKET

The stock market is a place where people buy and sell shares of stock. Shares are pieces of ownership in a company. Share prices rise and fall based on a company's strength. Prices may also fall when investors worry about the economy. Usually, share prices change slowly. But sometimes, they rise or fall quickly. On October 19, 1987, the stock market fell faster than it ever had before. It was a crash. People called it Black Monday.

Traders mill about the floor of the New York Stock Exchange as the stock market drops, October 19, 1987. In one day, stocks lost about 23 percent of their value.

This photo of the trading floor of the American Stock Exchange in New York, October 1987, shows the many computers used to trade stocks. After the crash, financial experts determined that computer programs which automatically sold stocks when their value dropped made the crisis worse.

Stock market crashes were not new. In 1929, share prices fell sharply for several days. That crash marked the start of the Great Depression. (The Great Depression was a ten-year period of economic chaos. It was the worst financial disaster in U.S. history.) The 1987 crash happened even faster. On Black Monday alone, the stock market lost nearly one-fourth of its value. Some people wondered if another depression was starting.

The Black Monday crash proved different from the one in 1929. After a few tense days, share prices began to rise again. No depression followed. The stock market slowly returned to normal. Even today, nobody is certain what caused the Black Monday crash.

Marching students carry a sign asking for greater democracy in China, April 1989.

BLOODSHED IN CHINA

The 1980s were a fateful time for many communist nations. In 1985, Soviet leader Mikhail Gorbachev began making changes. He started allowing more freedoms in the Soviet Union. Other communist countries soon followed. However, China was different. When Chinese citizens demanded change, their government said no. In 1989, China's army killed hundreds of protestors. The incident is known today as the Tiananmen Square massacre.

A large portrait of Mao Zedong overlooks Tiananmen Square in China's capital, Beijing. Mao established a communist government over China in 1949. He ruled the country until his death in 1976.

China first became communist in 1949. The move followed a long and bloody civil war. For decades afterward, China's communist government strictly controlled the lives of its people. They had little freedom. There were no free elections. Citizens were not permitted to criticize the government. The country's economy was also planned and controlled by the government. The economy suffered as a result. Food and other products were scarce. Most people were poor.

In the 1980s, China began making small changes to its communist system. The government gave up a little bit of its control over the economy. It also began experimenting with free elections at the local level.

Chinese people liked the reforms and wanted more. College students were especially vocal about further changes. A government official named Hu

A Chinese man blocks a line of tanks headed toward Tiananmen Square, June 5, 1989. This heroic act, recorded by television cameras, captured the world's imagination.

Chinese students duck behind cars as a truck carrying soldiers passes on patrol, June 7, 1989. The actual death toll during the government crackdown is unknown. Estimates of the number of Chinese protesters killed range from two hundred to five thousand.

Yaobang was their hero. He wanted more reforms too. Hu Yaobang died in April 1989 of a heart attack. Thousands of students turned out to mourn his passing.

The students gathered at Tiananmen Square. It is a public place in the Chinese capital of Beijing. In the days that followed, more students came to Tiananmen Square. They were joined by Chinese workers. The large crowd began demanding an end to communism in China. The nation's communist leaders refused. Protests at Tiananmen Square grew larger and louder. By May, more than 100,000 students and workers were marching on the square each day. Protests had also sprung up in other Chinese cities.

By early June, however, the crowds at Tiananmen Square had shrunk. Only about two or three thousand students continued to occupy the square.

China's communist leaders decided to end the protests. They sent the army to clear Tiananmen Square. Tanks and at least 10,000 soldiers surrounded the square on June 3. The students were ordered to disperse. On the morning of June 4, according to Western eyewitnesses, the students filed out of Tiananmen Square peacefully. But soon afterward, Chinese soldiers began firing at students and residents of Beijing who supported the students. The violence continued for several days. Hundreds of people were killed. Thousands more were injured.

For months, the Chinese government continued its crackdown. Many protestors were tracked down and arrested. Some were executed. Chinese officials banned foreign news reporters. The progress gained from China's reforms was lost. Many nations condemned the Tiananmen Square massacre. In China, it remains a forbidden subject even today.

Bloodshed in China

CULTURE OF GREED

America's economy steadily improved during the 1980s. The struggles of the 1970s were over. Many people were able to earn more money at work. For some, making money became an obsession. They always wanted more wealth, and would do nearly anything to get it. These businesspeople created a culture based on greed.

The 1987 movie *Wall Street* aptly portrayed the culture of greed. Michael Douglas played the film's villain, who was a ruthless investor. He said, "Greed,

Oliver Stone's 1987 film *Wall Street* was a critical look at the corporate culture of the 1980s. One of the film's most famous lines, "greed . . . is good," was spoken by actor Michael Douglas's character, a corporate raider named Gordon Gecko (left). The Gecko character was modeled in part on real-life bond trader Michael Milken.

Wall Street trader Ivan F. Boesky (center) made millions by investing in companies that were about to be taken over by corporate raiders. After a government investigation, Boesky admitted that he had illegally been given secret information about the companies before he purchased their stock. Boesky spent two years in prison and was fined $100 million.

for lack of a better word, is good." Although fictional, the villian was based on real-life people known as corporate raiders. They used their wealth to take over companies. Corporate raiders sought only to make money for themselves. Often their actions harmed the company and its workers.

At the time, greedy investors were viewed as smart businesspeople. However, it soon became clear that some of them were cheating. Stock trader Ivan Boesky pleaded guilty to fraud in 1986. Real estate investor Leona Helmsley was convicted of tax evasion in 1989. In 1990, bond investor Michael Milken was sentenced to ten years in prison for illegal trading. Their criminal acts showed the dangers of greed. People lost respect for the corporate raiders and other selfish investors.

Billionaires Harry and Leona Helmsley enter a federal court in New York to face tax evasion charges, 1988. Harry Helmsley was not healthy enough to stand trial, so Leona had to face the charges alone. She was convicted in 1989 and spent eighteen months in a federal prison.

On June 12, 1987, President Reagan gave a speech in front of the Brandenburg Gate in West Berlin. He challenged the Soviet Union to allow greater freedom in the countries of Eastern Europe, demanding, "Mr. Gorbachev, tear down this wall!"

THE BERLIN WALL FALLS

The Soviet Union was breaking apart. It had once been a powerful empire. Yet by the late 1980s it was slipping into chaos. For decades, the Soviet government controlled many smaller nations in Eastern Europe. Those countries began declaring their independence. In 1989, East Germany took a dramatic step toward freedom. German citizens knocked down the Berlin Wall. It was a visible symbol of the Cold War. The concrete wall divided the German city of Berlin in half.

This sign marked Checkpoint Charlie, a point in the Berlin Wall where people were permitted to cross between East Berlin and West Berlin—provided their paperwork was in order.

After losing World War II, Germany was split into two separate nations. East Germany fell under Soviet rule. West Germany remained free. The capital city was split into East Berlin and West Berlin. People living in East Berlin were subject to harsh communist rule. Those in West Berlin enjoyed free and comfortable lives. Before long, unhappy residents in East Berlin began moving to the other side of the city.

By 1961, more than two million people had fled East Germany. In response, communist officials put up barbed wire and a twelve-foot wall. It was designed to keep people from slipping into West Berlin. Guards patrolled the

Residents of East and West Berlin meet after a section of the Berlin Wall at Potsdamer Platz is knocked down, November 12, 1989.

Today, graffiti-covered sections of the Berlin Wall are on display in many places as memorials to the Cold War. The German text on this section reads, "What counts is to tear down many walls."

wall to ensure that no one climbed over it. For twenty-eight years, the Berlin Wall separated the city. Some East Germans continued trying to escape to West Berlin. At least eighty died during the attempt.

By 1989, East Germany's communist government had grown weak. It relied on support that the Soviet Union could no longer give. East German citizens were pleased. They were eager to shed communism and rejoin West Germany. In November of that year, they began tearing down the Berlin Wall. The guards did not try to stop them. The East Germans cheered as each slab of concrete fell. They proudly walked across the border into the western half of the city.

East and West Germany reunited as a single, free nation in 1990. The Soviet empire was crumbling. Countries such as Hungary, Poland, and Romania were also breaking away. Soviet leader Mikhail Gorbachev had accidentally started an amazing chain of events. Gorbachev hoped to make the Soviet Union stronger. Instead, his reforms led to its downfall. The Soviet Union officially ceased to exist in 1991. It split into fifteen separate nations. The Cold War was over.

U.S. Troops Invade Panama

Panama is a country in Central America. It is home to the Panama Canal, which connects the Atlantic and Pacific oceans. During the 1980s, a ruthless dictator ruled Panama. His name was Manuel Noriega. For six years, Noriega bullied his people and ignored the law. Finally in 1989, U.S. forces invaded Panama. Their goal was to capture and arrest Manuel Noriega, who was wanted in the United States for drug trafficking.

America and Panama share a long history together. The United States helped Panama gain independence from Colombia in 1903. Afterward, between 1904 and 1914, the United States built the Panama Canal. As part of a lease arrangement with Panama, America was given control of a ten-mile-wide strip of land that included

American soldiers parachute into a drop zone outside the city of David in western Panama, December 1989. Operation Just Cause, the U.S. invasion of Panama, was intended to protect Americans living in Panama as well as to stop the flow of illegal drugs into the United States.

An American Blackhawk helicopter passes over a ridge during a flight over Panama, 1989.

the canal. In the decades that followed, however, the two countries often argued about the canal. In the 1970s, America agreed to turn it over to Panama at the end of the century.

When Manuel Noriega first rose to power in 1983, America supported him. However, his actions quickly proved alarming. Noriega rigged elections. He used violence to silence his opponents. In 1988, a U.S. court charged Noriega with drug trafficking. U.S. president George H. W. Bush tried to force the Panamanian dictator to resign. When that failed, Bush ordered an invasion of Panama. American troops swept into the country and captured Noriega. They brought him to Florida, where he was tried and sent to prison.

DEA agents escort General Manuel Noriega onto a U.S. Air Force aircraft, January 1990. After his capture, the former Panamanian leader was flown to the United States and tried for drug trafficking.

Looking Ahead

A s the 1980s came to a close, a huge shift in global affairs was under way. The Soviet Union was collapsing, and Moscow's grip on the countries of Eastern Europe had loosened. In those countries, people were demanding more freedom, democracy, and an end to communism. By the early 1990s, Eastern Europe's communist regimes would all be replaced—and the Soviet Union itself would no longer exist.

The Cold War was over. Many people hoped that a new era of peace and democracy would begin.

Unfortunately, new conflicts would erupt in the 1990s. In some cases, the roots of these wars lay in events of the previous decade. Yugoslavia, a country in southeastern Europe made up of many ethnic groups, had been held together in part by the threat of a Soviet takeover. With the collapse of the Soviet Union, that threat no longer existed. In the early 1990s, simmering ethnic resentments in Yugoslavia exploded into civil war.

Iraq's long war with Iran during the 1980s left it deep in debt to other Arab countries, including Kuwait and Saudi Arabia. Iraqi dictator Saddam Hussein wanted his war debts forgiven. When the Arab countries refused, Saddam ordered an invasion of Kuwait. American troops were rushed to Saudi Arabia to protect that country from further Iraqi aggression. Later, in the Gulf War, a U.S.-led international force defeated Iraq and liberated Kuwait. But Saddam remained in power, and American troops remained in Saudi Arabia. Both situations would cause trouble for America throughout the 1990s and beyond.

Other trends in the 1990s were more positive. Personal computers became more and more powerful. Increasing numbers of people bought PCs. And the rise of the Internet made possible new ways of learning, sharing information, and doing business.

As the world's lone superpower, the United States intervened in several foreign conflicts during the 1990s. One was the Persian Gulf War, in which the United States organized an international coalition to reverse Iraqi dictator Saddam Hussein's invasion of Kuwait. Here, soldiers pose with Arabs holding the flags of Saudi Arabia and Kuwait after coalition forces liberated Kuwait in March 1991.

CHRONOLOGY

1980—In February, the U.S. Olympic hockey team upsets the heavily favored Soviet team. In November, Republican Ronald Reagan defeats Democrat Jimmy Carter in the presidential election.

1981—Iran releases its American embassy hostages in January. In March, John Hinckley Jr. attempts to assassinate President Reagan. The first space shuttle launches in April. MTV goes on the air.

1982—The Falklands War begins in March. In August, troops from America and other nations go to Lebanon in the hopes of stopping the fighting there.

1983—Astronaut Sally Ride becomes the first American woman in space. U.S. forces invade the Caribbean island of Grenada in October. In Lebanon, two suicide attacks on October 23 kill about 300 peacekeeping troops.

1984—Apple introduces its Macintosh computer in January. Teenager Ryan White is diagnosed with AIDS. He becomes a symbol of the growing epidemic. Ronald Reagan is reelected president in November.

1985—Mikhail Gorbachev becomes leader of the Soviet Union in March. He and President Reagan meet for the first time in November. Microsoft releases the first version of its Windows operating system.

1986—The space shuttle *Challenger* explodes shortly after takeoff in January. Teacher Christa McAuliffe is among those killed. In April, the Chernobyl nuclear accident occurs in Soviet Ukraine.

1987—The U.S. stock market crashes in October. In America, the crack cocaine epidemic reaches its peak.

1988—The Iran-Iraq War ends in August with more than a million casualties. George H. W. Bush is elected president in November.

1989—China's Tiananmen Square massacre occurs in June. East German citizens begin tearing down the Berlin Wall in November. U.S. forces invade Panama in December.

GLOSSARY

activist—A person who works to advance an idea or cause.

AIDS—A disease that weakens the body's ability to fight off other diseases.

armada—A large group of vessels that moves together.

Cold War—A struggle for global dominance between the United States and the Soviet Union that lasted from the late 1940s until 1991.

communism—A type of government in which all citizens are supposed to work for the good of society and share property equally.

corporation—A business or other organization that exists as its own legal entity.

crisis—A situation that has reached a critical and often dangerous stage.

economy—The system by which money and goods flow through society.

embassy—A building for representatives of a foreign country.

epidemic—The outbreak of an infectious disease.

investor—A person who commits money with the intent of making more money.

NASA—The National Aeronautics and Space Administration, America's space agency.

nuclear—Relating to energy that comes from the splitting or merging of atoms.

radiation—Invisible but harmful rays given off by nuclear materials.

scandal—A disgraceful incident that draws public attention.

superpower—An extremely powerful country, especially one that leads other countries.

trafficking—The trading or transporting of an illegal substance.

Further Reading

Bobek, Milan, editor. *Decades of the Twentieth Century: The 1980s*. Pittsburgh, Pa.: Eldorado Ink, 2005.

Jefferis, David. *Flight into Orbit*. New York: Crabtree Publishing, 2007.

Parker, Vic. *Chernobyl 1986: An Explosion at a Nuclear Power Station*. Chicago, Ill.: Heinemann-Raintree, 2006.

Roleff, Tamara L. *Cocaine and Crack*. San Diego, Calif.: ReferencePoint Press, 2007.

Sandler, Michael. *Hockey: Miracle on Ice*. New York: Bearport Publishing Company, 2006.

Schmemann, Serge. *When the Wall Came Down: The Berlin Wall and the Fall of Soviet Communism*. New York: Kingfisher, 2007.

Sebag-Montefiore, Hugh. *China*. New York: DK Eyewitness Books, 2007.

Simons, Rae. *AIDS & HIV: The Facts for Kids*. Vestal, N.Y.: AlphaHouse Publishing, 2008.

Sutherland, James B. *Ronald Reagan*. New York: Viking Juvenile, 2008.

Internet Resources

<http://www.hq.nasa.gov/office/pao/History/sts51l.html>
This page from NASA links to dozens of sites about the *Challenger* disaster. Learn details about how the accident happened, and how America honored the *Challenger* crew.

<http://www.newseum.org/berlinwall/>
An online exhibit about the Berlin Wall, this site includes photos and a timeline. It also describes life in East Germany during the Cold War.

<http://www.ryanwhite.com/>
Read the story of Ryan White, the boy who was diagnosed with AIDS at age 13. This official site includes text from speeches Ryan gave in 1988, just two years before his death.

Index

Operation Just Cause, 54
Operation Urgent Fury, 25

Panama, 54–55
Persian Gulf, 23, 56–57

Quinn, Martha, 18

Reagan, Nancy, 27
Reagan, Ronald, 4, 7, 24, 50
  and the Cold War, 20–21
  election of, 10, 12–13
  and Grenada invasion, 25
  and the Iran-Contra Affair,
    40–41
  shooting of, 14–15
  and the "war on drugs," 27
Regan, Don, 41
Resnik, Judy, 32

Rubik's Cube, 7
Run-D.M.C., 19

Saudi Arabia, 56
Scobee, Dick, 32
Shultz, George, 41
Smith, Mike, 32
Soviet Union, 5, 8–9, 20–21,
  25, 45
  and Afghanistan, 6, 21, 23
  breakup of the, 4, 6–7,
    51–53, 56
  and the Chernobyl disaster,
    36–39
space shuttles, 16–17, 32–33
sports, 6
  Olympics, 5, 8–9
stock market, 42–43
  See also economy

Stone, Oliver, 48

Taylor, Elizabeth, 28
technology
  personal computers, 5,
    30–31, 56
Three Mile Island, 37–38
"Thriller" (video), 19
Tiananmen Square
  massacre, 45, 46–47
Top Gun (movie), 35

Wall Street (movie), 48–49
Weinberger, Caspar, 41
West Germany, 51–53
White, Ryan, 29

Young, John W., 16, 17
Yugoslavia, 56

PICTURE CREDITS